LIVE ALL F(

MW00957182

OF CHRIST:

EXEGESIS OF COLOSSIANS

3:12-17

BY

JEFFREY J. LEE

WRITTEN: FRIDAY, MARCH 12 , 2011

PREFACE

The following writing is an expositional study of the book of Colossians 3:12-17 which focuses on how Christians must become more like Jesus Christ. Appendix A has a sermon included as an outworking and application of the message of this passage of Scripture. I was personally challenged by the reminder, that as a Christian, I need to continually focus and adapt my life to become more like Jesus. Besides, when we think of what we know of Jesus, who would not like to imitate him.

God Bless,

Rev. Jeffrey J. Lee

Table of Contents

INTRODUCTION: THE CHRISTIAN RESPONSE TO CHRIST: LIVE ALL FOR THE GLORY OF CHRIST

Since the formation of the church on the day of Pentecost there have been challenges among Christians within the church. Disagreements, arguments, criticism, sin and much more have been the cause of much conflict in the church. This is the reason that the Apostle Paul wrote the church in Colosse, to help Christians in Colosse to focus on Christ and living for the glory of Christ amidst the many challenges that they face from people inside and outside the church. The real issue was that there were false teachers in the church causing challenges and judging each other. Warren Wiersbe once said, "Wrong doctrine always leads to wrong living. Right doctrine should lead to right

---

[1] Wiersbe, W. W. (1996). *The Bible exposition commentary* (Php 4:14). Wheaton, Ill.: Victor Books. (Logos Bible Software)

living."[1] Paul is writing to correct the wrong way of living

by focusing on the one who helps Christians live right,

Jesus Christ!

BACKGROUND

THE CITY OF COLOSSE

Colosse was an ancient city that was located along the fertile river valley next to the river Lycus.[2] Colossae was a vibrant city many years before the book of Colossians was written. The city had lost prominence over the years leading up to the writing of the book of Colossians due to the expansion and growth of the city of Laodicea which was within a short distance of Colosse. The major trade route from "Ephesus and Sardis to the Euphrates"[3] originally went through Colosse but later moved north and away from the city. The city was home to a large wool industry. There was a large regional

---

[2] Elwell, W. A., & Comfort, P. W. (2001). *Tyndale Bible dictionary.* Tyndale reference library (299). Wheaton, Ill.: Tyndale House Publishers. (Logos Bible Software)

[3] O'Brien, P. T. (2002). *Vol. 44: Word Biblical Commentary : Colossians-Philemon.* Word Biblical Commentary (p. xxvi). Dallas: Word, Incorporated. (Logos Bible Software)

3

earthquake in AD. 60 – 61 that also may have had a devastating effect on the community and larger area.[4] The city was also very multicultural as many areas were represented include a large Jewish population. Josephus, a historian of the time, wrote about that "Antiochus III brought two thousand Jewish families from Babylon and Mesopotamia and settled them in Lydia and Phrygia."[5] This meant that the area had a strong Jewish influence that will also culturally affect the Christian church as it is established in Colosse.

CONTEXT OF THE PASSAGE

LARGER CONTEXT

---

[4] O'Brien, P. T. (2002). *Vol. 44*: *Word Biblical Commentary : Colossians-Philemon*. Word Biblical Commentary (p. xxvi). Dallas: Word, Incorporated. (Logos Bible Software)

[5] O'Brien, P. T. (2002). *Vol. 44*: *Word Biblical Commentary : Colossians-Philemon*. Word Biblical Commentary (p. xxvii). Dallas: Word, Incorporated. (Logos Bible Software)

The church in Colosse was not a direct church plant by Paul the Apostle. Paul established a thriving work in Ephesus which no doubt had an effect on the province of Phrygia which included the cities of Laodicea and Colosse. MacArthur agrees saying, "The man who founded them was not Paul, since he included the Laodiceans and Colossians among those who had never seen him in person (2:1)."[6] What we do know is that Epaphras was the one who shared Christ in Colosse as recorded by Paul say, " because of the hope laid up for you in heaven. Of this you have heard before in the word of the truth, the gospel, which has come to you, as indeed in the whole world it is bearing fruit and growing—as it also does among you, since the day you heard it and understood the grace of God in truth, just as you learned it from Epaphras our beloved

---

[6] John MacArthur, *Colossians* (Chicago: Moody Press, 1996) (Logos Bible Software)

fellow servant. He is a faithful minister of Christ on your behalf." Colossians 1:5–7 (ESV).

Epaphras went to visit Paul, in Rome, while he was in prison. He reported to Paul the commendable things the church was doing such as their example of faith and their love for other Christians.[7] There were however some challenges facing this church from within and without. There is an indication that the church may have struggled with a positive testimony to the larger community of Colosse as Paul said, "Walk in wisdom toward outsiders, making the best use of the time." Colossians 4:5 (ESV) The church of Colosse, like many other churches at the time, was being exposed to issues of false teaching. Epaphras was so concerned by these influences that he made the trek to Rome which was over a thousand miles to get the Apostle Paul's advice and wisdom in the matters.[8]

---

[7] Colossians 1:4

[8] John MacArthur, *Colossians* (Chicago: Moody Press, 1996) (Logos

There was the introduction of early Gnostic teachings of gaining greater knowledge and denied the deity of Christ.[9]

There was a Jewish influence on the church that was encouraging Christians to follow some of the legalistic teachings of the Old Testament. There is the issue of circumcision which Paul deals with in (2:11-15) by teaching a new type of circumcision that was not of the body but a spiritual circumcision through faith in Christ and symbolized in baptism. Paul also deals with the issue of special days of celebration and worship. No doubt many Gentile Christians had kept some of the cultural holidays and may have moved to meeting on the first day of the week, which was a Sunday, and had been regularly practiced but not legislated by the Apostles (Acts 20:7; 1 Cor 16:2). The Jewish people historically and culturally

---

Bible Software)

[9] John F. Walvoord, ed., and Roy B. Zuck, ed., *The Bible Knowledge Commentary* (Colorado Springs: Chariot Victor Publishing, 1983), p. 677.

kept the Sabbath because it was instructed by the Lord for his people in the Ten Commandments. Also, the issue of eating different kind of foods would have been a challenge for Jews because there were regulations in the Old Testament that restricted eating certain animals. This issue would have posed great challenges to the church. However, Paul deals with special Cultural days, Sabbaths and food in teaching the Colossians, "Therefore let no one pass judgment on you in questions of food and drink, or with regard to a festival or a new moon or a Sabbath." Colossians 2:16 (ESV) Paul's instructions were not to judge each other that there is freedom to worship different times of the week and eat all foods. He also teaches on these issues in greater depth in Romans 14.

Paul the Apostle also speaks to the issue of the Colossians view of Christ. As mentioned earlier, there was an issue within the Gnostic teach that taught that denied the deity of Christ. Much of the book of Colossians deals with the supremacy of Christ over all things. This is exemplified in the Paul's clear teaching in Colossians 1:15 when he said of Christ that, "He is the image of the invisible God, the firstborn of all creation." Peter O'Brien, in his commentary on Colossians said, "Paul's statements about the uniqueness and supremacy of Christ's work in creation and redemption (1:15–20) are a reminder that they need look nowhere else than to Christ for a completion of salvation and his exhortations are to be understood as general warnings."[10] The importance of the teaching of Christ, his life and supremacy are very important to the context of Colossians 3:12-17.

IMMEDIATE CONTEXT

---

[10] O'Brien, P. T. (2002). *Vol. 44*: *Word Biblical Commentary : Colossians-Philemon*. Word Biblical Commentary (xxxi). Dallas: Word, Incorporated.

Paul starts Colossians 3:12 with the word Ἐνδύσασθε (endyo) which means "to put on, clothe"[11] oneself. Here in this context the second person, plural, imperative which means that Paul was commanding the Colossian Christians to clothe themselves, to put on the following traits that he will discuss. But also just as important is the conjunction οὖν (oun) which literally is translated then, consequently or therefore. The thought is, "expressing either simple sequence or consequence,"[12] which means that Paul is saying, consequently, after what I have instructed you of previously, put what I am going to tell you into practice. Paul has in 2:6-15 described, to the Colossian Christians, the fact that Jesus Christ is supremely above all creation and all things. In 2:16-23, that same Jesus Christ, because he is rules supremely, has authority to

---

[11] Wesley J. Perschbacher, ed., *The New Analytical Greek Lexicon* (Peabody, Massachusetts: Hendrickson Publishers, Inc., 1990), 142.
[12] (Perschbacher, 1990), 299.

release from legalism. Christ has called Christians in 3:1-4 to focus upon him and his heavenly kingdom because they have died with him and have been raised to new life with him at his φανερόω, which literally means bring to light, make an appearance, reveal.[13] The apostle Paul said, "When Christ who is your life appears, then you also will appear with him in glory." He reminds the church, even through the challenges, through difficulties that their destiny is glory through Christ and with Christ! The life of each believer is to live for the glory of the all supreme ruler of life, Jesus Christ. The importance of all this leads into Paul's point in 3:5-11 in which he wants the church to do the opposite of 3:12 and "put to death (νεκρόω - nekroo)" the list of attitudes and actions he presents. The term "put to death" can also convey the following meaning, "to cease completely from activity, with the implication of extreme

---

[13] (Perschbacher, 1990), 425.

measures taken to guarantee such a cessation—'to stop completely, to cease completely."[14] Paul contrasts the lists in 3:5,8 with a positive list of attitudes to "clothe" themselves with. These attitudes and actions are in keeping with the one who believes and follows Christ.

[14] Louw, J. P., & Nida, E. A. (1996). *Vol. 1*: *Greek-English lexicon of the New Testament : Based on semantic domains* (electronic ed. of the 2nd edition.) (660). New York: United Bible societies), 524.

COMMENTARY

Analysis of Colossians 3:12-17

> *Living Like Christ (3:12)*
>
> *Forgiving Like Christ (3:13)*
>
> *Loving Like Christ (3:14)*
>
> *Living in the Peace of Christ (3:15)*
>
> *Responding to the Word of Christ (3:16-17a)*
>
> *Living all for Christ (3:17b)*

Living Like Christ (3:12)

The context in 3:12 leads Paul to command the Colossian church, "As God's chosen ones," to literally (Ἐνδύσασθε root ἐνδύω - endyo) clothe, put on the actions and attitudes that he teaches. The ESV and NKJV uses, "put on" which is a literal rendering. However, the majority of reference to ἐνδύω in the New Testament has to do with clothes, wearing them and putting them on like

Paul's teaching to the Romans to "clothe yourselves with the Lord Jesus Christ." (Rom 13:14) The Greek-English lexicon of the New Testament defines ἐνδύω (endyo) in this way, "to put on clothes, without implying any particular article of clothing."[15] The NIV seems right then to have translated this passage, "clothe yourselves." The reason for this is that the in English, "put on" can have a reference to put belongs is a particular place as well as doing such tasks as putting on a pair of shoes. The word Ἐνδύσασθε (endysasthe) is in the middle voice which is defined as, "the subject does the action of verb in some way that concerns itself."[16]

The NIV seems to indicate this idea better in English because Paul is instructed them to put on the

---

[15] Louw, J. P., & Nida, E. A. (1996). *Vol. 1*: *Greek-English lexicon of the New Testament : Based on semantic domains* (electronic ed. of the 2nd edition.) (524). New York: United Bible societies.
[16] Willam Mounce, *Greek for the Rest of Us* (Grand Rapids: Zondervan, 2003), 148.

particular attitudes (3:12b). Not to put on the attitudes just anywhere but to clothe themselves, their lives with these attitudes. The word Ἐνδύσασθε (endysasthe) is also in the imperative which means that Paul is not just suggesting that the Colossian Christians do this, but it is an instruction from God, through his directly appointed apostle, to embody in their lives "compassionate hearts, kindness, humility, meekness, and patience." (3:12)

Paul uses the term οὖν (oun) which is a conjunction is important to this passage because it conveys "deduction, conclusion, summary, or inference to the preceding discussion."[17] The evil vices that are described in (3:5,8) are to be "put to death or kill,"[18] and now Paul lists for the church a list that he commands to clothe themselves with. It is interesting that he uses this term because what a person

---

[17] Heiser, M. S. (2005; 2005). *Glossary of Morpho-Syntactic Database Terminology.* Logos Bible Software.
[18] (Perschbacher, 1990), 282.

wears can speak outwardly of their likes and dislikes. Clothing such as a uniform can differentiate a nurse from a police officer, or a fireman from a soldier. Here Paul wants the Colossians to identify with these attitudes and actions that are in keeping with how Jesus Christ lived. Paul uses the same word ἐνδύω in Romans 13:14 when he says to the Roman Christians, "But *put on* the Lord Jesus Christ, and make no provision for the flesh, to gratify its desires." (italics added) The consistency of Paul's teaching in this area indicates these traits are of Christ. Therefore, in clothing themselves with the traits of "compassionate hearts, kindness, humility, meekness, and patience," they are clothing themselves with the clothes of Christ. The challenge is for the Colossians to live like Christ. This is in keeping with Paul's next words which he uses to describe Christians as those who are, "God's chosen ones" (3:12) as those who are "holy and beloved" (3:13). Paul is reminding the Colossians that the lifestyle in keeping with "God's chosen, they "have put off the old self with its practices and have put on the new self, which is being renewed in knowledge after the image of its creator" (3:9-10). The word ἐκλεκτός (eklektos), which means "chosen as a recipient of special privilege, elect."[19] ἐκλεκτός (eklektos) is an adjective that identifies with the noun "God's" along with the plural form which means that Christians are God's chosen one's or people. The ESV uses the word "chosen ones." The NIV uses "chosen people" which is different the NKJV which uses "the elect of God." The term "chosen people" in this case is the best way to understand what Paul is communicating because "chosen" has more of a definitive nature then the word elect. In many democracies, people are elected in and out of government and there is a time frame. Election has a

---

[19] (Perschbacher, 1990), 128.

revolving sense.   Whereas, God's choosing a people is definitive, not revolving as taught by Paul (2Cor 5:5), "He who has prepared us for this very thing is God, who has given us the Spirit as a guarantee."   The word ἐκλεκτός (eklektos) is also in the plural form that indicates more than one person, therefore the NIV rendition is best when it says, and "God's chosen people."   O'Brien said, "Believers are "God's elect" (ἐκλεκτοὶ θεοῦ - eklektos Theu) against whom he will never lay any charge for it is he who justifies them (Rom 8:33)."[20]   The work of choosing a people for himself is God's and it he who determines who is justified as his own.   There is under-tones of the Old Testament name of the Israel as "God's chosen" now being passed

---

[20] O'Brien, P. T. (2002). *Vol. 44: Word Biblical Commentary : Colossians-Philemon.* Word Biblical Commentary (198). Dallas: Word, Incorporated.

[21] Kenneth L. Barker and John R. Kohlenberger III, ed., *The Zondervan NIV Bible Commentary: Volume 2: New Testament* (Grand Rapids: Zondervan Publishing House, 1994), 835.

onto the church as God's holy and loved. Barker and Kohlenberger said, "The three terms... emphasize the favored position now enjoyed by Christians as heirs of Israel's privileges."[21]

Paul does not stop in describing who Christians are as God's chosen people. He states that they are also "holy and beloved, ἅγιοι καὶ ἠγαπημένοι (agioi kai egapenenoi)." The word ἅγιοι is defined as "pertaining to being holy in the sense of prior moral qualities and possessing certain essentially divine qualities in contrast with what is human—'holy, pure, divine."[22] Because ἅγιοι (agioi) is an adjective it is connected to the word "God's" which means that along with Christians being God's choose people they are also defined as holy. We are not made holy on our own put through the work of God, a fact recorded in Hebrews

[22] Louw, J. P., & Nida, E. A. (1996). *Vol. 1: Greek-English lexicon of the New Testament : Based on semantic domains* (electronic ed. of the 2nd edition.) (744). New York: United Bible societies.

which says, "(Heb 10:10 ESV) And by that will we have been sanctified through the offering of the body of Jesus Christ once for all."

The word ἠγαπημένοι (egapemenoi) is defined as "to love, value, esteem, feel or manifest generous concern for, be faithful towards; to delight in."[23] This is how God looks at each of his chosen people while genuine and generous love. Paul is teaching the Colossian Christians that as God's people, he loves them dearly, they are of great value. The verb tense is in the perfect which is, "a completed verbal action that occurred in the past but which produced a state of being or a result that exists in the present."[24] In the perfect tense ἠγαπημένοι (egapemenoi) describes that each Christian is loved by God (Eph 1:4–5 ESV) "he chose us in him before the foundation of the

---

[23] (Perschbacher, 1990), 128.
[24] Heiser, M. S. (2005). *Glossary of Morpho-Syntactic Database Terminology*. Logos Bible Software.

world, that we should be holy and blameless before him. In love he predestined us for adoption as sons through Jesus Christ, according to the purpose of his will." In love God chose, predestined, his people to be holy and blameless. The idea of being chosen by God has often created controversy because it may seem stiff and unloving yet as Dr. John MacArthur, pastor and theologian, said, "Election is not a cold, fatalistic doctrine. On the contrary, it is based in God's incomprehensible love for His elect."[25] The ESV, NASB, NKJV all translated ἠγαπημένοι as beloved, however, the NIV translated it as "dearly loved." The NIV is grasping the idea that God's chose are not just loved but there is a deeper love, hence "dearly loved" is a better translation of the idea Paul is attempting to teach.

Paul moves on to describe the Christ-like qualities that each Christian needs to envelop. He begins with

---

[25] (John MacArthur, 1996), 153.

σπλάγχνα οἰκτιρμοῦ (splagchna oiktirmou) which literally means chief intestines or bowels[26] but is a figurative expression that is defined as the centre of the emotions, which is the heart.[27] The word οἰκτιρμοῦ (oiktirmou) denotes the emotion of compassion or sympathy.[28] There is a sense of deep emotional feeling of compassion within our hearts. The ESV translates σπλάγχνα οἰκτιρμοῦ (splagchna oiktirmou) as "compassionate hearts," and NIV just "compassion," while the NKJV uses, "tender mercies." While the NIV uses the idea of compassion, it seems to have missed the deeper aspect of the emotions, heartfelt compassion that is indicated in the Greek. The NKJV use of tender mercies is a good understanding of the mercy and tenderness that Christians must live out in Christ. The ESV

---

[26] (Perschbacher, 1990), 128.

[27] (P.T. O'Brien, 2002), 199.

[28] *Vol. 5: Theological dictionary of the New Testament.* 1964- (G. Kittel, G. W. Bromiley & G. Friedrich, Ed.) (electronic ed.) (159). Grand Rapids, MI: Eerdmans.

best describes the meaning in the use of "compassionate hearts." Paul wanted the Colossian Christians to understand that their first task is to be compassionate people like their Saviour, Jesus Christ

The next quality of a Christian must be χρηστότητα (chrestoteta) which literally is means kindness or goodness.[29] The Colossian Christians were to exemplify an attitude and life of kindness toward others and within their disposition. It is also one of the fruits of the Spirit mentioned in Galatians 5:22.

Added to the qualities of compassionate hearts and kindness is the quality of humility (ταπεινοφροσύνην - tapeinopsrosunen). In stark contrast to the false teachers within and without the church who were prideful, Paul calls the Colossians to live in humility as Christ did. In James

---

[29] (Perschbacher, 1990), 440.

4:10 he instructs Christians to, "Humble yourselves before the Lord, and he will exalt you."

Next, Paul commands the quality of πραΰτητα which is literally gentleness or meekness.[30] A definition with greater clarity is, "gentleness of attitude and behavior, in contrast with harshness in one's dealings with others."[31] The ESV and NKJV translate πραΰτητα as "meekness," but the NIV uses "gentleness." Both are correct, but the term gentleness would be greater understood in current culture. Gentleness is also one of the fruit of the Spirit listed by Paul in Gal 5:22 and must exist as part of the life of every Christian.

The last quality that Paul shares in 3:12 is the quality of μακροθυμίαν (makrothumian), patience. There

---

[30] (Perschbacher, 1990), 342.

[31] Louw, J. P., & Nida, E. A. (1996). *Vol. 1*: *Greek-English lexicon of the New Testament : Based on semantic domains* (electronic ed. of the 2nd edition.) (748). New York: United Bible societies.

may have been a tendency among Colossian Christians toward impatience toward each other amidst the false teachings that were impacting the church. O'Brien writes about this when he said, "It denotes that 'longsuffering' which endures wrong and puts up with the exasperating conduct of others rather than flying into a rage or desiring vengeance."[32] Paul calls Christians to live patiently in with others.

The Colossian Christians were to clothe themselves with these five qualities as God's chosen people. This is part of living the new life in Christ that Paul shares in 3:10. Living for Christ includes throwing off the clothes of the old self and clothing themselves with new clothes that show compassion, kindness, humility, gentleness and patience.

---

[32] O'Brien, P. T. (2002). *Vol. 44: Word Biblical Commentary : Colossians-Philemon.* Word Biblical Commentary (201). Dallas: Word, Incorporated.

Forgiving Like Christ (3:13)

Paul moves from instructions on the attitudes and qualities that are expected of those who follow Jesus Christ to how they were to react when wronged by others. Paul states in 3:13 that they were to bear with one another and to forgive each other. Pauls starts off by using the word ἀνεχόμενοι (anechomenoi) which means literally "to endure patiently"[33] and is in the present tense which means that the process is ongoing, that it does not have a end. Paul is making sure that there is no question as to how Christians are to react to other people, with ongoing patience. They were not to endure with each other, for a short time but always. This is best indicated in the ESV and NKJV which translate the word ἀνεχόμενοι (anechomenoi) as bearing, which gives that sense of ongoing patience. The NIV uses the phrase "bear with

---

[33] (Perschbacher, 1990), 29.

each other," but does not give the sense of continuous patient endurance.

Paul answers the question that might arise by the Colossians next in regard to someone hurting them, sinning against them or offending them as he said, "bearing with one another and, if one has a complaint against another, forgiving each other." The word "*momphe* (μομφή), denotes "blame"[34] in the form of a complaint. The idea is, if one has a complaint, in which they could blame another party, they were to endure patiently with person or group of people and also "forgive" them. The use of the word μομφή by the NIV to define it as "grievance" does not find itself being used major literal sources for its definition but it is a logical interpretation of the word into English as it is defined as, "a real or imagined cause for complaint."[35]

[34] Vine, W. E., Unger, M. F., & White, W. (1996). *Vol. 2: Vine's Complete Expository Dictionary of Old and New Testament Words* (117). Nashville, TN: T. Nelson.
[35] Soanes, C., & Stevenson, A. (2004). *Concise Oxford English*

Complaining can be both real and imagined, but in the case of this passage it is not defined either way. It is general complaining.

The reaction of the Colossians was χαριζόμενοι (chapizomenoi) which could be defined as giving generously, to forgive or to cancel a debt. Cαριζόμενοι (chapizomenoi) is in the future tense which denotes that forgiving is continuous. The pronoun ἑαυτοῖς (eautois) is reflexive and plural so in means that they need continuously be "forgiving yourselves."[36] When it comes to the challenges of living and working with others, the Colossians were not to seek trouble, reprisal or vengeance but to continually forgive each other, to free the other from their debts, complaints, anything that they held against them.

---

dictionary (11th ed.). Oxford: Oxford University Press.

[36] MacArthur, J. (1996). *Colossians* (156). Chicago: Moody Press.

The reason that Paul gives the Colossians to forgive is not based on subjective reasoning but on the objective reality of what God has supremely done through Christ. Again, the theme that Paul puts across in Colossians is that life is all about Christ. Paul said, "As the Lord has forgiven you, so you also must forgive." The Colossians needed to clothe themselves with the five qualities found in 3:12 and continue by clothing themselves with the forgiveness of Christ. Christians marked by a life of forgiveness as exemplified by Christ. The word ku,rioj (kurios) within the context of this passage refers to Christ. In 3:17; 24 Paul joins kuri,ou (kurios) ,Ihsou/ (Iesou) as Lord Jesus and seems to inference the fact that we are forgiven our sins and debts by Christ. O'Brien said in regard to 3:13, "Because Christ has forgiven us we ought to forgive one another. κύριος (kurios) ("Lord") is the better attested reading and refers to Christ himself rather than God."[37] In 1 Peter 2:20 – 20, we are told of the example of Christ when it comes to the wrong done to us by others, *"For what credit is it if, when you sin and are beaten for it, you endure? But if when you do good and suffer for it you endure, this is a gracious thing in the sight of God. For to this you have been called, because Christ also suffered for you, leaving an example, so that you might follow in his steps."* Christ is the ultimate example of forgiveness for the Christian, he is the example that Paul wants the Colossians to live by.

LOVING LIKE CHRIST (3:14)

The Colossians are also commanded to (epi pasin de toutois) ἐπὶ πᾶσιν δὲ tou,toij (and to all these things supervene upon)[38] or add to these "love." Paul wants that Colossians to understand that the greatest thing to clothe

---

[37] O'Brien, P. T. (2002). *Vol. 44: Word Biblical Commentary : Colossians-Philemon.* Word Biblical Commentary (202). Dallas: Word, Incorporated.

[38] (Perschbacher, 1990), 159.

themselves with, enveloping all the other qualities, is the quality of love. Love in 3:14 is conveys the idea "to have love for someone or something, based on sincere appreciation and high regard—'to love, to regard with affection, loving concern, love."[39] Christians are to ultimately clothe themselves with a great love, affection and respect for their Christian family and toward outsiders. In Colossians 4:5, Paul said, "Walk in wisdom toward outsiders, making the best use of the time." The word tou,toij (toutois) is a demonstrative pronoun, plural, which convey the fact that all the nouns that Paul has just listed that are qualities for the Colossian Christians to clothe themselves with, the greatest single quality is ἀγάπην (agapen), love. The ESV, NKJV and NIV agree with by stating, "put on love." However, the NIV adds the word

---

[39] Louw, J. P., & Nida, E. A. (1996). *Vol. 1*: *Greek-English lexicon of the New Testament : Based on semantic domains* (electronic ed. of the 2nd edition.) (292). New York: United Bible societies.

"virtues" most likely in attempt to help the reader understand that love is not just added to the past qualities or virtues but is "over all these virtues" they are to "put on love." In the context of the current challenges that the Colossian Christians may face both inside and outside the church, along with the current false teaching controversy that had begun in the church, Paul wants the believers to clothe themselves with love. The thing which, su,ndesmoj (sundesmos) binds, bundles, fastens or unites things together) in τελειότητος (teleiotetos) (perfect, complete) harmony is love. The NKJV keeps a word for word parody using the phrase, "which is the bond of perfection." The ESV uses "binds everything together in perfect harmony," and NIV uses, "binds them all together in perfect unity." The NIV is making and interpretive assumption that love binds together all the virtues just listed in the passage. The ESV on the other hand is taking a interpretive position that

32

love "binds everything together in perfect harmony." This means that the translators are taking the position that love leads to perfection. D.A Carson said, "The words 'of perfection' probably, however, denote purpose: love is the bond that leads to perfection. It binds together the members of the congregation (rather than the graces of v 12) into unity in the body of Christ so producing perfection."[40] This is the best interpretation of the passage because the phrase in the original Greek, ὅ ἐστιν σύνδεσμος τῆς τελειότητος stands on its own as it says literally, "which is a bond of perfection." It also relates to where Paul is going in 3:15 where he said, "indeed you were called in one body." Paul wanted the Colossians to know that above all qualities mention in 3:12-13 that love is above them all and that love unifies and binds them together toward perfection and

---

[40] Carson, D. A. (1994). *New Bible commentary : 21st century edition* (4th ed.) (Col 3:12–17). Leicester, England; Downers Grove, Ill., USA: Inter-Varsity Press.

maturity as a community of believers which is a part of the sanctification process (Heb 2:10-11).

LIVING IN THE PEACE OF CHRIST (3:15)

The Colossians were now to continue to clothe themselves with Christ's peace. The word βραβευέτω (brabeneto) literally is "to preside, direct, rule, govern, be predominant."[41] They were to let the peace of Christ direct and rule their lives. This is in contrast with those prideful and self-seeking false teachers and Judaizers who would not allow the love and peace of Christ to rule their lives. The idea of peace is not emotional sense of peace but a peace that is present with us through the work of Christ.[42] (Ephesians 2:14), "For he himself is our peace, who has made us both one and has broken down 'in his flesh the

---

[41] (Perschbacher, 1990), 74.

[42] Carson, D. A. (1994). *New Bible Commentary : 21st century edition* (4th ed.) (Col 3:12–17). Leicester, England; Downers Grove, Ill., USA: Inter-Varsity Press.

dividing wall of hostility." Paul commands the Colossians to let the peace of Christ rule over their lives, as heart here refers to the "center of one's personality as the source of will, emotion, thoughts and affections." [43] and also includes the fact that they all ἐκλήθητε (eklethete) , called as a community of Christians into this sphere of peace.[44] Paul continues further to clarify for those who may have been responding to his teaching negatively that they are to καὶ εὐχάριστοι γίνεσθε (kai eucharistoi), which means and be thankful! The verb γίνεσθε (ginesthe) is in the imperative which means that thankfulness is not an option but a command. In reality this is the very purpose of the Christian's existence is to be thankful. Paul reminds the

---

[43] O'Brien, P. T. (2002). *Vol. 44*: *Word Biblical Commentary : Colossians-Philemon.* Word Biblical Commentary (204). Dallas: Word, Incorporated.

[44] Carson, D. A. (1994). *New Bible commentary : 21st century edition* (4th ed.) (Col 3:12–17). Leicester, England; Downers Grove, Ill., USA: Inter-Varsity Press.

Colossians that their heart attitude must be clothed in thanksgiving. They must thankfully live in the peace of Christ in all things.

RESPONDING TO THE WORD OF CHRIST (3:16-17a)

The (logos) logos (word) of Cristou/ (Chistou) refers to the Gospel of Jesus Christ that first came to the Colossians through Epahras (Col 1:7).[45] In light of those who were denying the deity of Christ and worshiping angels, Paul goes straight to the matter by explaining whose message and by whose authority the Colossians are to "dwell" in, that is Jesus Christ. The word of Christ is the final authority for all (Phil 2:9-11). His word spoke the world and universe into being (John 1:3). Paul commanded the Colossians to allow this word to (enoikeo) e.noike,w,

---

[45] O'Brien, P. T. (2002). *Vol. 44*: *Word Biblical Commentary : Colossians-Philemon.* Word Biblical Commentary (206-207). Dallas: Word, Incorporated.

literally "dwell in, inhabit"[46] their lives. Those who are true followers of Christ will obey and follow Christ's word and will continually (e.noike,w – enoikeo is in the present form) allow it to take up residence in their lives to mature them. Also, plousi,wj (phousios) mean richly or also abundantly. The idea is that Christ's word would fill their lives greatly to overflowing.

Paul goes on to explain how this must happen, how the word of Christ was to indwell them richly. First it was to affect their knowledge (σοφία - sophia wisdom, knowledge). Paul's prayer was for the Colossian to, "filled with the knowledge of his will in all spiritual wisdom and understanding (Col 1:9)." The early Gnostics prided themselves on knowledge and wisdom put is all foolishness when it comes to the wisdom and knowledge of Christ (1 Cor 3:19). Paul wants the Colossians to focus on knowing

---

[46] (Perschbacher, 1990), 145.

Christ and His word, which is true wisdom. This was to be done through teaching and admonishing each other, which is important because the Colossians may have sensed that they were not to correct or teach or challenge each other. The context of all this is important because in 3:14 love was to be the overall attitude of believers. This means speaking the truth in love (Eph 4:15). True love will desire to humbly with love admonish (νουθετοῦντες nouthetountes – admonish, instruct or warn) and teach. This also included all forms of worship starting with teaching then singing psalms, hymns and spiritual songs. The NIV uses, "songs from the Spirit," which is an interpretation that the songs of the early church where based on the Old Testament. However, the word πνευματικαῖς (pneumatikais) is literally "spiritual." There were obviously psalms and hymns from Scripture but there were most likely songs that developed in the early church that would be classed a spiritual songs that were not necessarily inspired by the Holy Spirit, though there is obviously influence of the Holy Spirit. D.A. Carson said, "*Psalms, hymns and spiritual songs* is a broad expression and includes OT psalms, liturgical hymns as well as spontaneous Christian songs."[47] The teaching, admonishing and singing, are all apart of Christian worship within the context of the local church and must be characterized by "thankfulness in your hearts to God." The word χάριτι (chariti) is literally "grace." The ESV uses, "thankfulness," while the NKJV uses, "grace." The NIV tries to use the word "gratitude," tries to capture the idea that the Colossians were to be both gracious and thankful in their worship of God. John MacArthur said, "Perhaps its use here encompasses both ideas: believers sing out of

---

[47] Carson, D. A. (1994). *New Bible commentary : 21st century edition* (4th ed.) (Col 3:12–17). Leicester, England; Downers Grove, Ill., USA: Inter-Varsity Press.

thankfulness for God's grace."[48] Paul wanted the Colossian believer to respond to the word of Christ to be clothed in worship with thankfulness and grace.

LIVING ALL FOR CHRIST (3:17b)

The climax of this passage is fitting with the theme of Colossians focusing Christ. He wants the Colossians to pursue living for Christ continuously (ποιῆτε poiete – do or make is in the present voice). Paul said, "And whatever you do, in word or deed, do everything in the name of the Lord Jesus (3:17)." He wants the Colossians to know that in all the challenges, in all problems in life both inside and outside the church, they are to do all for the name of Jesus Christ, with thankfulness! In John 3:35-36, Jesus said, "The Father loves the Son and has given all things into his hand. Whoever believes in the Son has eternal life;

---

[48] MacArthur, J. (1996). *Colossians* (159). Chicago: Moody Press.

whoever does not obey the Son shall not see life, but the wrath of God remains on him." Jesus wants Christians to obey him; this is in keeping with what a true Christ follower must be. This is a help and a test of the Colossian Christians, Those who truly follow Christ will live differently in the world. Christians must live wholeheartly for Jesus Christ.

THEOLOGICAL POINTS

THEOLOGICAL POINTS

1. Paul calls the church at Colosse, "chosen ones, holy and beloved." The church is God's people; he has chosen it by grace as his own.

2. Christ is by the Holy Spirit dwells in the heart of each believer but must be present in their life which includes emotions, thoughts, will and body.

3. Christ, in the context of this passage, is the one who has forgive believers for their sin and debts.

4. The Colossian believers where to live and work for the glory of Christ.

5. Thankfulness is the response of the Christian to God.

APPLICATIONS

1. For Churches

    a. The church is the chosen people of God. They have received the inheritance and privileges of Israel.

    b. Church is to exemplify compassion, kindness, humility, patience, forgiveness, love, thankfulness in all they do.

    c. Churches are to forgive other churches.

    d. Worship of God is to be focused on Him and includes many different forms.

    e. Love must accompany teaching and admonition.

    f. Do all things for the glory of Christ

2. Individuals

a. Christians must clothe themselves with the compassion, kindness, humility, patience forgiveness and love.

b. Christians are commanded to forgive each other because of Christ's forgiveness of them.

c. Love is to reign supreme in the attitude of the Christian believer.

d. The word of Christ must live in abundance in the Christian.

e. Worship is a necessity, not an option for the Christian.

f. Christ-like living and giving glory to Christ is the ultimate goal of each Christian.

g. Be thankful to God in all things.

APPENDIX A

SERMON

TITLE: How to live for the glory of Christ?

TEXT: Colossians 3:12-17

INTRODUCTION

Secular Illustration: Interview with BBC talk show host about the death of body builder who used steroids. Peer pressure was the main issue.

Personal Transition: Do you feel that there are pressures in life caused by the bigger society to do something that may be harmful to your health, life? How about church? Are their influences inside and outside the church that are attempting to pull you away from what it the right way to live (reference secular illustration – succumbed to pressure)

Biblical Transition: The Christians in the church of Colosse back during the Apostle Paul's day were facing challenges to give up in their Christian life and give in to the false teaching that was growing in popularity. Warren Wiersbe once said, "Wrong doctrine leads to wrong living."

Proposition: Paul reminds the Christian believers in Colosse that their task is to live for the glory of Christ no matter what happens in their personal or church life.

Interrogative Sentence: How are you to live for the glory of Jesus Christ today in light of your struggles and pressures to compromise your faith?

Transitional Sentence: There are three keys to living for the glory of Jesus Christ that Paul shares with the Colossians for you to follow.

1. Your life must reflect living for Christ

   a. Living for Christ – five qualities

i. As God's people you must embody these five qualities (elaborate)

ii. Illustration – Illustration (being in Poland and seeing clothing that looked like it was authentically Nike/Reebok and other big names but on closer inspection finding they were fake when you looked at the names on the tags they read Niike and Reebeek! On close inspection we can see what is real and what is not.

iii. Christians on close inspection can be seen as authentic or not by using this test in 3:12 and further on.

iv. Romans 3:14

v. Are you living out these qualities in your life? How do you measure up?

b. Forgive like Christ

    i. Forgiveness and enduring with each other are not optional within the church. You are commanded to forgive and patiently endure.

    ii. Illustration – Have you every though the wrong impression of someone and gone off your rockers, only to find out that you were wrong later. Sometimes people are just have a bad day. We don't know may have happened to that other person to spark an argument or attitude.

      iii.   You are called to a life clothed with forgiveness and patience toward others.

      iv.   How are you doing when it comes to showing forgiveness to your wife, husband, children, mom or dad, neighbour, pastor, etc?

c. Loving like Christ

      i.   Paul wanted the Colossians to not only forgive and be patient with each other but also show love. Love is what brings about unity and harmony in the church and the life of an individual.

      ii.   On a scale of one to ten... how is your love meter when it comes to loving others? Do you listen to

others in need? Are you looking for
opportunities to show love
practically toward others?

d. Living in the Peace of Christ

    i. Those who are always attempting to
get their own way, prideful, arrogant
can cause great destruction in the
church and in lives of individuals

    ii. Paul wanted the Colossian Christians
to live in the peace of Christ. Christ
has set us free from sin and from the
punishment of God. We must allow
Christ, and his peace to rule over our
lives

    iii. Eph 2:14

    iv. Are you allowing Christ to control
your life?

2. Your life must follow the word of Christ

    i. Paul wanted the Colossians to let the word of Christ, the gospel and teaching to live and take up residence in their in abundance. Showing love in teaching and admonishing each other. This includes the areas and forms of worship. Christ's Word must reign supreme in the Christians life.

    ii. Illustration – Eating plan I am on. I was sceptical at first but after results and feeling good I bought into it. Christ wants us to buy into the live the he is has given to us, to "live for him in word and deed."

iii. Are you content in following and living in the word of Christ? To allow it to change you, mould you and shape you?

3. Live all for Jesus Christ

    i. Paul wanted the Colossians to focus, not on the problems and challenges of people, issues because we will always have those till the return of Jesus Christ. He wanted the Colossians to follow Christ in everything, all things!

    ii. John 3:35-36

    iii. Are you willing to live you live entirely for the Lord Jesus Christ, to focus fully on Him? This is our calling as Christians. It is our

destiny to live a Christ-like life.

CONCLUSION

C.T. Studd, the famous English cricketer and member of the English XI cricket team, gave away his vast wealth and became a missionary a century ago. His slogan was, "If Jesus Christ be God, and died for me, then no sacrifice can be too great for me to make for him.

Jesus Christ, you Saviour, the one who died for you to set you free from your sin and bring you to God calls you today to give up your all to live like him, to love like him, to forgive like him, and follow his word. We are his hands and feet to our world in need of hope today. Allow Christ to change you and see him change others through you as you live and love for him!

BIBLIOGRAPHY

Barker, Kenneth L., and Kohlenberger III, John R., eds.
The Zondervan NIV Bible Commentary. Grand
Rapids: Zondervan, 1994.

Carson, D. A. *New Bible Commentary: 21st century
edition* (4th ed.) (Col 3:12–17). Leicester, England;
Downers Grove, Ill., USA: Inter-Varsity Press,
1994.

Comfort, Philip., ed. *Life Application Bible Commentary.*
Wheaton, Illinois: Tyndale House Publishers, 1995.

G. Kittel, G. W. Bromiley & G. Friedrich, Ed. *Vol. 5*:
Theological dictionary of the New Testament.
(electronic ed.). Grand Rapids, MI: Eerdmans,
1964.

Heiser, M. S. *Glossary of Morpho-Syntactic Database
Terminology*, 2005. Logos Bible Software.

Louw, J. P., & Nida, E. A. *Vol. 1*: *Greek-English lexicon of
the New Testament : Based on semantic domains*
(electronic ed. of the 2nd edition.) New York:
United Bible Societies, 1996. Logos Bible
Software.

MacArthur, J. *Colossians*. Chicago: Moody Press, 1996.

Mounce, William D. *Greek for the rest of us.* Grand
　　Rapids: Zondervan, 2003.

O'Brien, P. T. *Vol. 44*: *Word Biblical Commentary :
　　Colossians-Philemon*. Dallas: Word, Incorporated,
　　2002 (Logos Bible Software)

Perschbacher, Wesley J. *The New Analytical Greek
　　Lexicon.* Peabody, Massachusetts: Hendrickson
　　Publishers, 1990.

Soanes, C., & Stevenson, A. *Concise Oxford English
　　dictionary* (11th ed.). Oxford: Oxford University
　　Press, 2004.

Vine, W. E., Unger, M. F., & White, W. *Vol. 2*: *Vine's
　　Complete Expository Dictionary of Old and New
　　Testament Words* (117). Nashville, TN: T. Nelson,
　　1996.

Walvoord, John F., ed., and Zuck, Roy B., ed. *The Bible
　　Knowledge Commentary.* Colorado Springs:
　　Chariot Victor Publishing, 1983.

Wiersbe, W. W. *The Bible exposition commentary* (Php
　　4:14). Wheaton, Ill.: Victor Books, 1996. (Logos
　　Bible Software)

About the Author

Jeffrey Lee is a Canadian, who works in his ancestral homeland of the United Kingdom, as a missionary, involved in church planting and church restoration ministries with ABWE Canada (Across Borders for World Evangelism). He is an ordained minister with the Fellowship of Evangelical Baptist Churches of Canada from the province of Ontario, were he was born and raised. He graduated with his B.R.E from Heritage College and Seminary in Cambridge, Ontario and is currently studying an M.Div with Liberty University in Lynchburg, Virginia. His passion is making the biblical Jesus known to the world, seeing them become committed and growing disciples of Christ. He has a love for the study of church history, the early church fathers and especially such figures as Augustine, Calvin and Luther, to name a few.

Made in United States
Troutdale, OR
12/17/2024

26799500R00037